The Whimsical World of Marion Wright

Art and Stories by Marion Wright

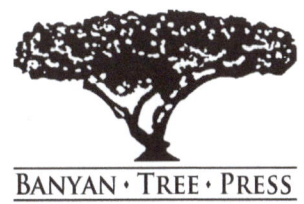

BANYAN · TREE · PRESS

The Whimsical World of Marion Wright:
Art and Stories by Marion Wright
© 2011 Marion Wright. All Rights Reserved.

No part of this publication may be reproduced or transmitted in any form or by any means, mechanical or electronic, including photocopying and recording, or by any information storage and retrieval system, without permission in writing from author or publisher (except by a reviewer, who may quote brief passages and/or show brief video clips in review).

ISBN: 978-1-936449-14-9
Library of Congress Control Number: 2011943915

Cover and Interior Design by: BPMediaPro.com

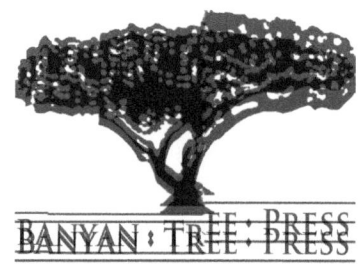

Banyan Tree Press
a subsidiary of Hugo House Publishers, Ltd.
Englewood, CO
Austin, TX
(877) 700-0616
www.BanyanTreePress.com
www.HugoHousePublishers.com

Dedication

This book is dedicated to my parents and brother, Bill, whose influences brought me to this point in my life. As a child I used to watch my father working on cuckoo clocks in our basement. He would often remove the cuckoos and replace them with something totally unexpected. You will notice that all my machine paintings have gears, wheels, and cogs which are reminiscent of that time so many years ago. My mother was artistic and had a fine appreciation for beauty. She and my father talked with my brother and me about art and took us to the Smithsonian as well as to art galleries and museums in Europe. I could not have produced my paintings or written this book without the influences of these wonderful people.

Table of Contents

Dedication iii
Introduction v
The American Bi Flycycle 3
The Bat and Broom Mobile 4
Cat Herding Machine 7
The Dream Review Machine 8
Fly by Night Rhinoceros 11
Gardening Robot in Love with Spade 12
Gertrude Ghostbuster and Her Collection of Friendly Spirits 15
The Great American Airhen 16
Jupiterian Musicians 19
The Magical Mystical Mooch Machine 20
Mother Goose's Robot 23
Much Ado About Nothing 24
The Portable Hole Processor 27
Robot in Love with Vacuum Cleaner 28
Snail in Love with Tape Dispenser 31
The Standing Assistance Machine for After a Nine Course Meal 32
Teenager from Mercury with QPXMA 35
The Tuck in Kiss Goodnight Machine 36
Two Women from Venus Wearing Elaborate Hats 39
Woman Wearing Elegant Hat 40
Woman with Bats in Belfry 43
Woman with a Screw Loose 44
Woman with Skeleton in Closet 47
Young Man with Hare on Chest 48
About the Author 50

Introduction

I have always loved art and writing but never thought seriously of putting them together into my own book. A few years ago friends started urging me to do this by saying, "Write a book about your art so you can show us your work! We want to know what your paintings are all about!" So I sat down to write "The Whimsical World of Marion Wright" and you are holding the results in your hands. I want you to know that I am deeply grateful to all of you for your encouragement, because I could not have done it without you.

I wish to express extreme gratitude to Dr. Patricia Ross and her team at Banyan Tree Press who worked so hard to get this book out, and to Kathy Hadsall of FMS Digital for her outstanding photography. I'm also exceedingly grateful to friends who proofread my writing and gave me so many excellent suggestions. I cannot thank all of you enough and I'm wishing you God's blessings and peace.

Marion Wright
Denver, Colorado 2011

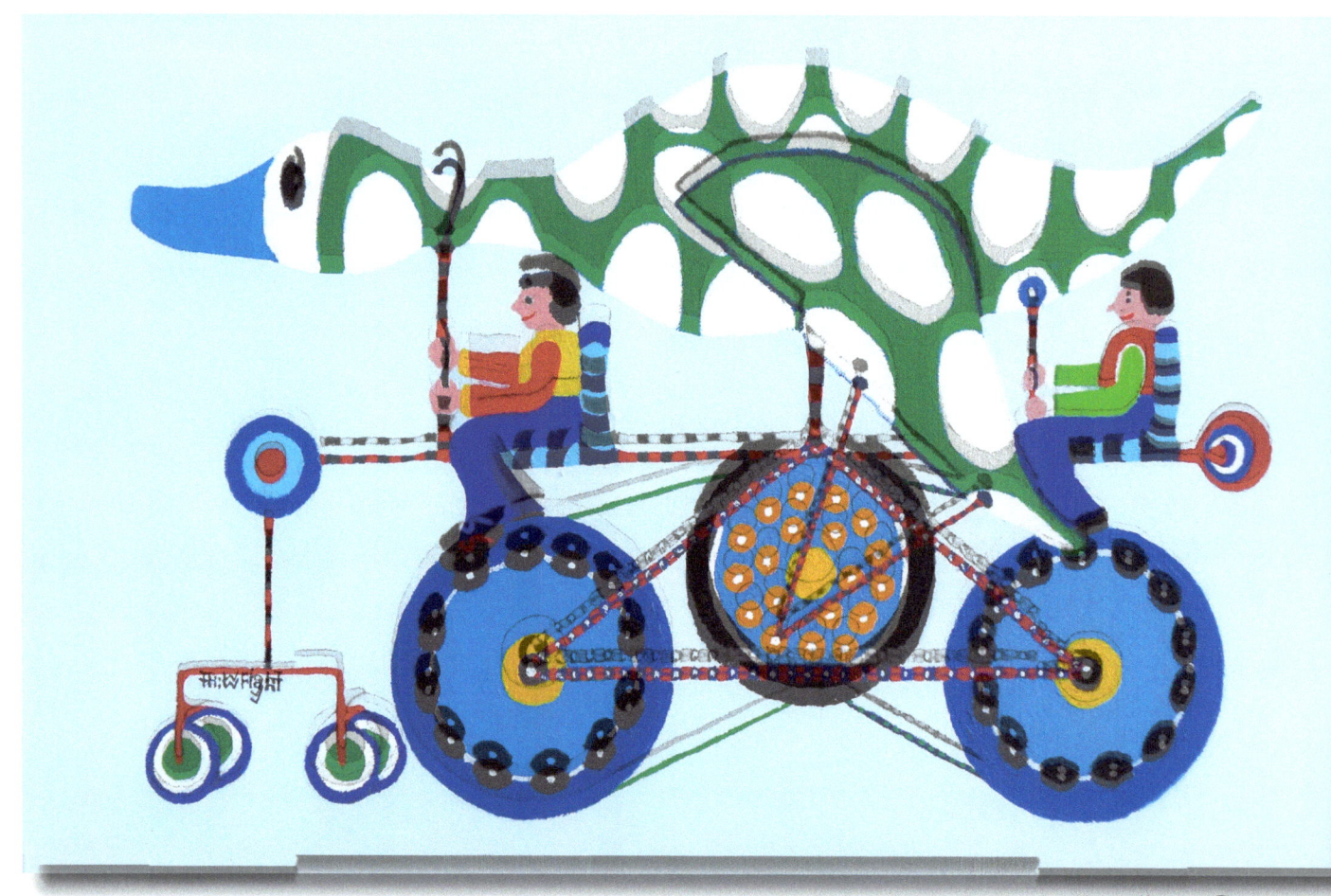

Acrylic on Canvas
15" X 24" - 1989

The American Bi-Flycyle

Two people pedaling in unison operate this most unusual flying machine. The large blue gears turn the red-spotted wheel, which controls the rate of speed and number of wing flaps. The operator in front controls the altitude by moving the head of the goose, while the operator in back controls the tail rod, which acts as a rudder. The four small green wheels in front are for landing and to protect the more fragile blue wheels. This machine is not difficult to fly, but operators need to concentrate and pedal at the same speed or the Bi-Flycycle may lose altitude or capsize.

The Bat and Broom Mobile

Older witches develop cataracts, glaucoma, and arthritis so it is difficult for them to ride their brooms, particularly at night.

Recently it was noted that the senior witch population has increased, and that they needed a vehicle for their non-broom-flying elders. As a result the coven purchased the Bat and Broom Mobile to be operated by younger witches. One witch turns the crank to activate the wings and adjusts the cable to move the head, while her companion uses the broom as a rudder. Passengers have a choice of riding on the top of the vehicle where the view is excellent, or in the gondola with the operators.

The Bat and Broom Mobile was an instant success with the older witches. Now they can go out and enjoy the fresh breezes and cool evening air without worrying about flying into trees, stepping on their robes, or tripping over rocks.

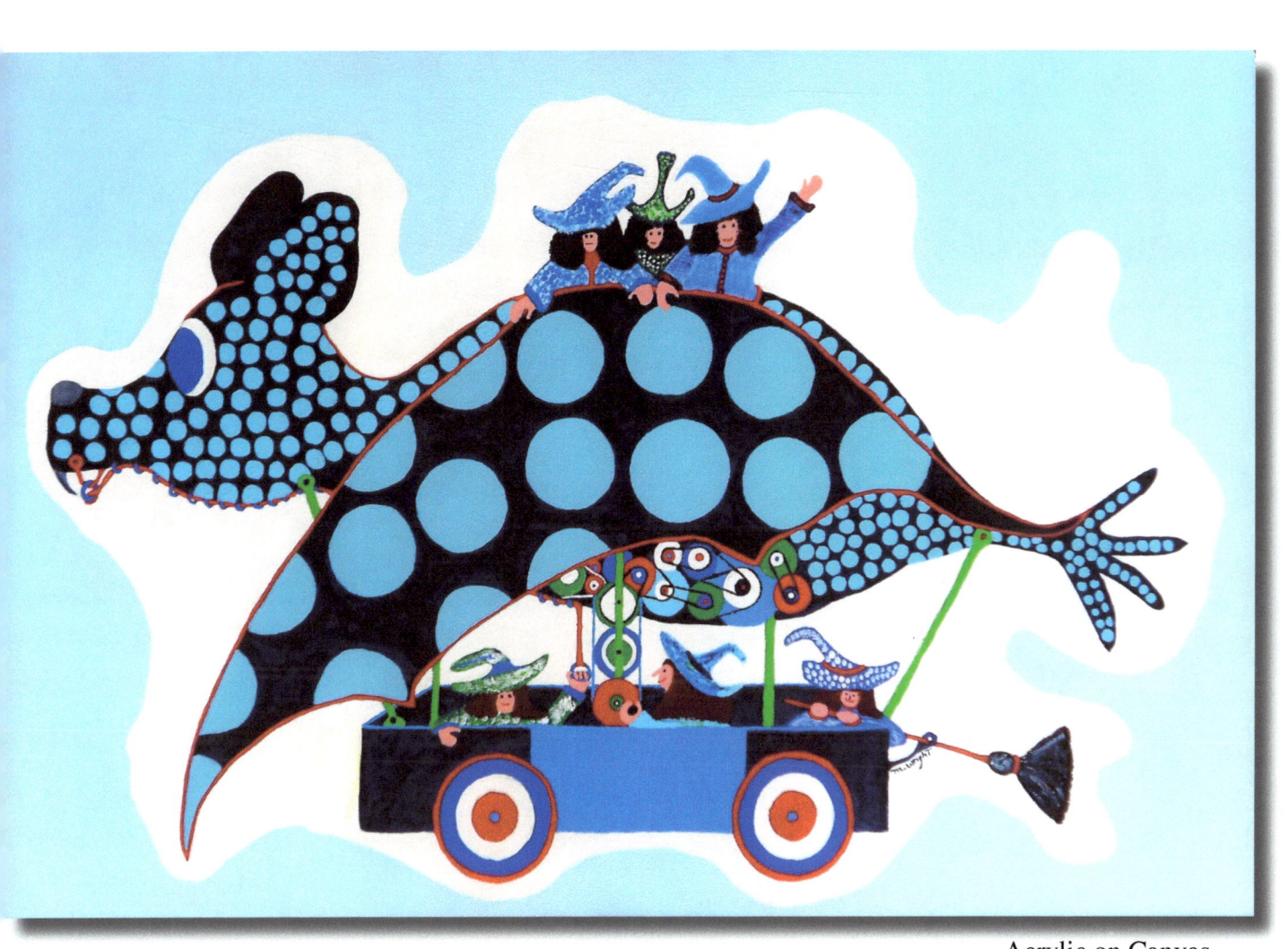

Acrylic on Canvas
24" X 36" - 1982

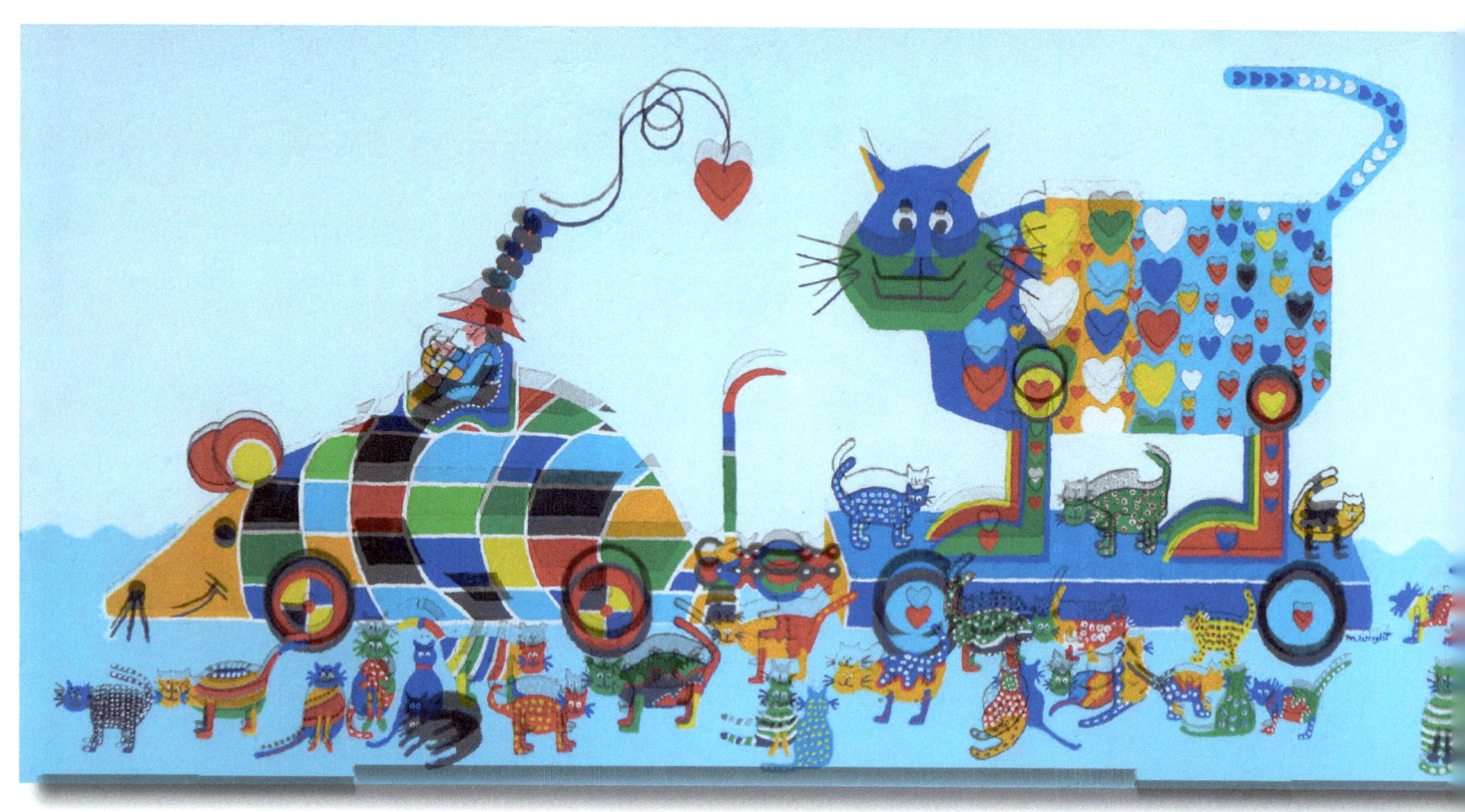

Acrylic on Canvas
24" X 48" - 2010

Cat Herding Machine

When a friend mentioned that getting a group of artists to agree on anything is "like trying to herd cats," I decided to design a cat-herding machine. I reflected that cats are notorious for being independent and they are definitely not a herd animal, so a machine that makes them go in the same direction might be useful. It seemed to me that since many of them are "mousers," they might follow a large and colorful cat cart drawn by a mouse-mobile. To entice them to the area, I put catnip in the big cat, but I never expected the results! Cats came running from every direction and followed the "herder," for miles! In the end I discovered that cats can be herded, but only if you provide the right environment and offer them something they cannot resist.

The Dream Review Machine

This machine is for people who are willing to share their dreams. This sleeping subject is wearing an electronic hat which transmits his dream into a computer where it will be stored in full color with sound and then put on a video. If needed, the computer can also print a description of the dream for backup.

In this case the dreamer, wearing a double hat and carrying an orange cone used to fix the streets, is being chased by a dragon. The dragon then turns into a bathtub made of flapjacks, which the dreamer and an unknown associate transform into a fig tree.

It will be very helpful to the subject to have another person see this dream exactly as it was created so it can be discussed in detail.

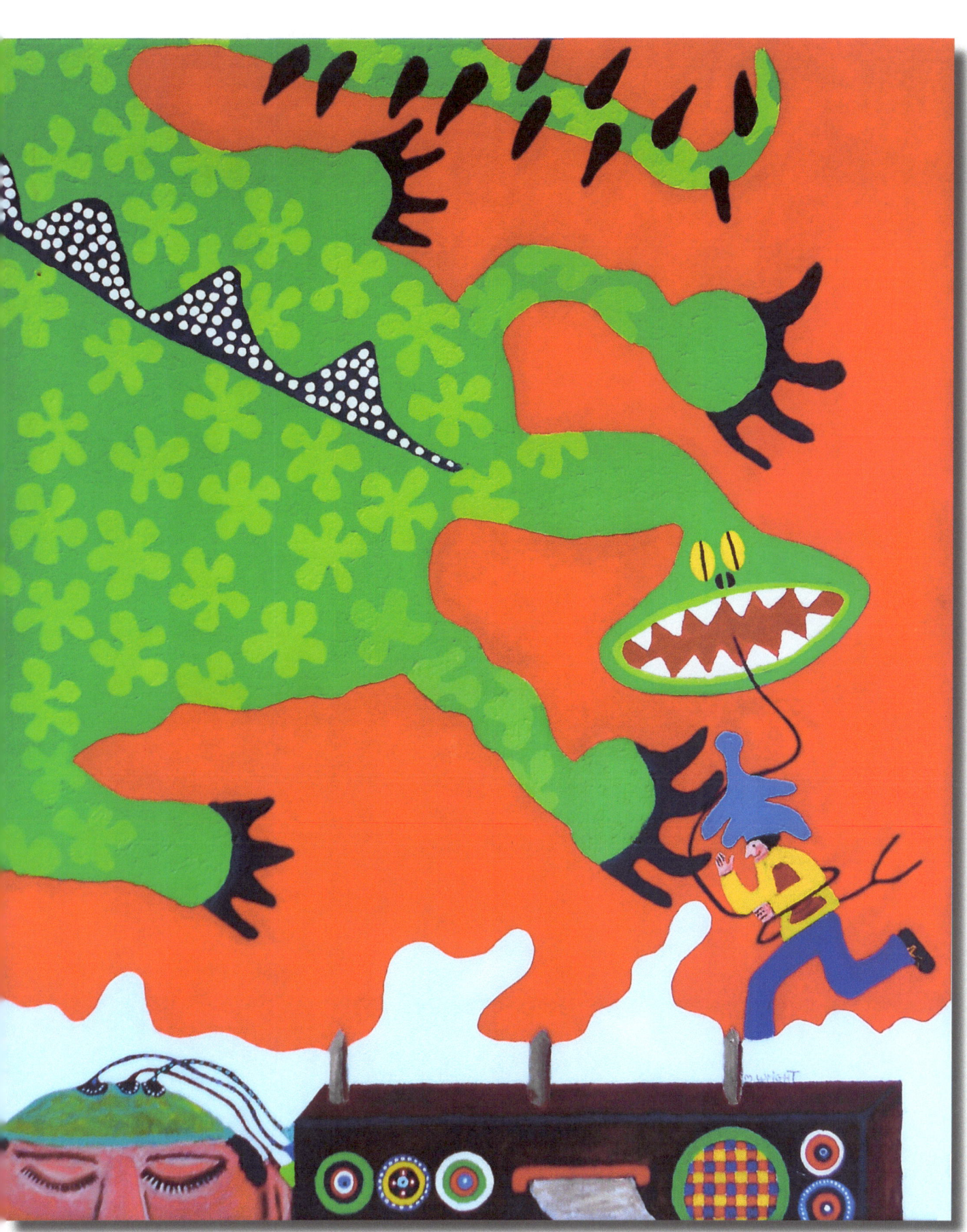

Acrylic on Canvas
30" X 36" - 1982

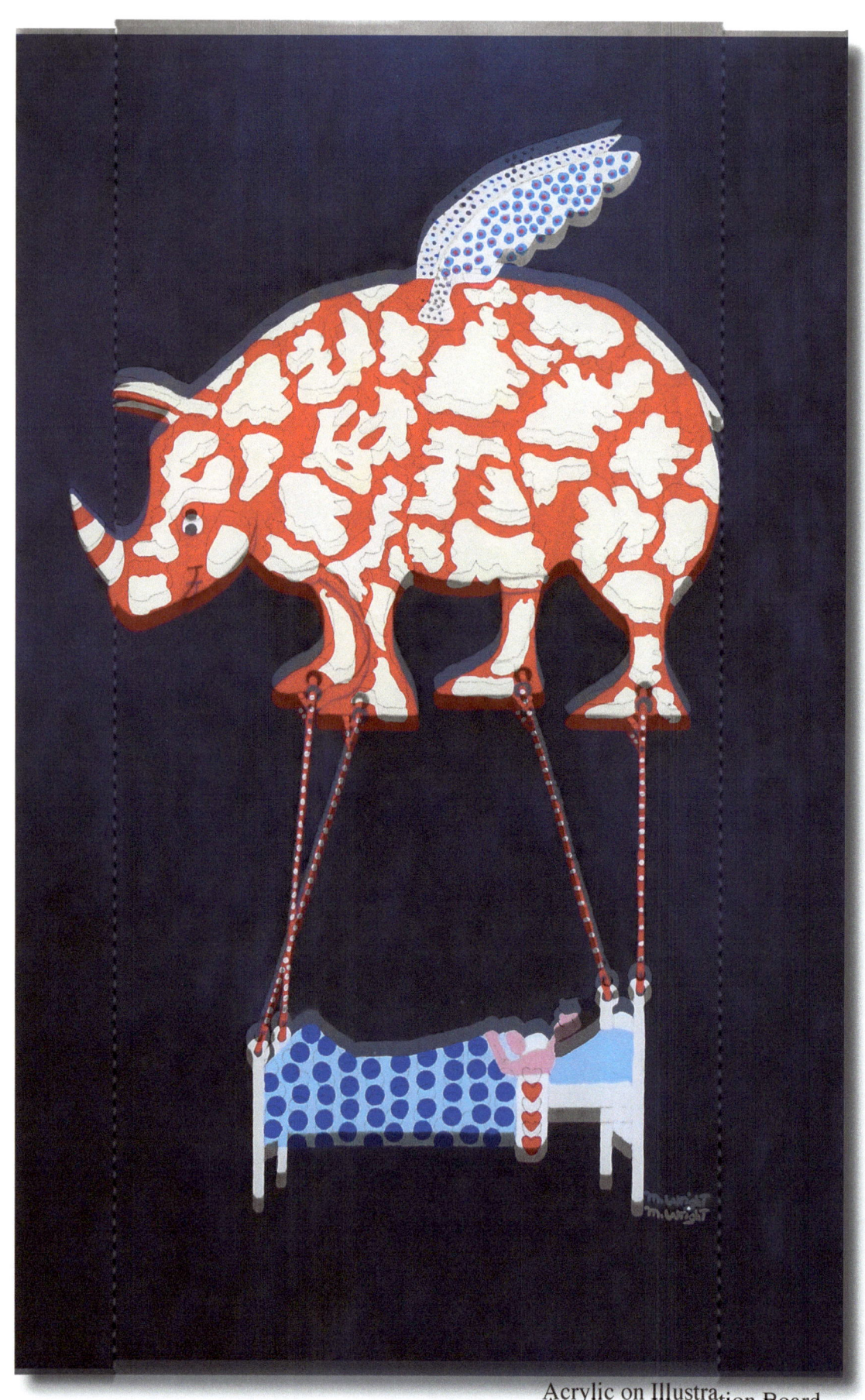

Acrylic on Illustration Board
20" X 30" - 2004

Fly By Night Rhinoceros

This flying rhinoceros searches for people who are having a hard time sleeping, and after hooking his feet to their bed, he flies them around the world. The gentle rocking motion of the flight lulls them to sleep, and the next morning they wake up at home without any memory of their voyage. When you have a good long sleep and wake up feeling restored and relaxed the next morning, it's possible you had a visit from this most unusual machine.

Gardening Robot in Love with Spade

This robot is named Arugula, and she is programmed to plant, water, weed, and fertilize your garden. She can work without instructions, but she understands orders and can follow directions well. Being a robot, Arugula never tires and will work from dawn to dusk without interruption.

The programmers who designed this robot gave her feelings of love so she would be gentle to all plants and animals, but they never bargained on romance! They were absolutely amazed to discover that she had fallen in love with her spade and named him "Doug"! At present Arugula cannot do her work because she is so deeply in love that all she can do is gaze at her spade. After all, who would want to stick their lover's head in the dirt?

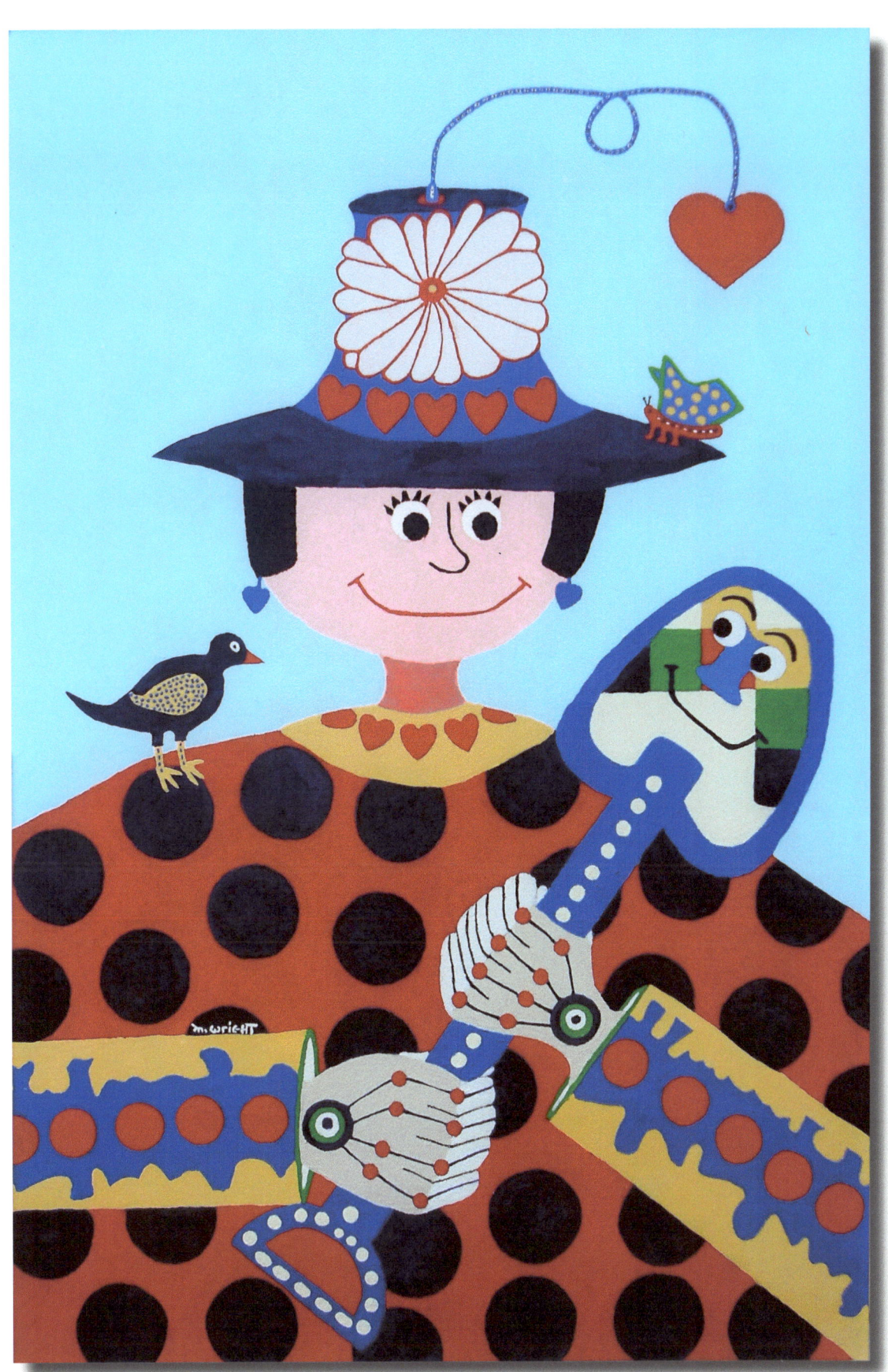

Acrylic on Canvas
24" X 36" - 2003

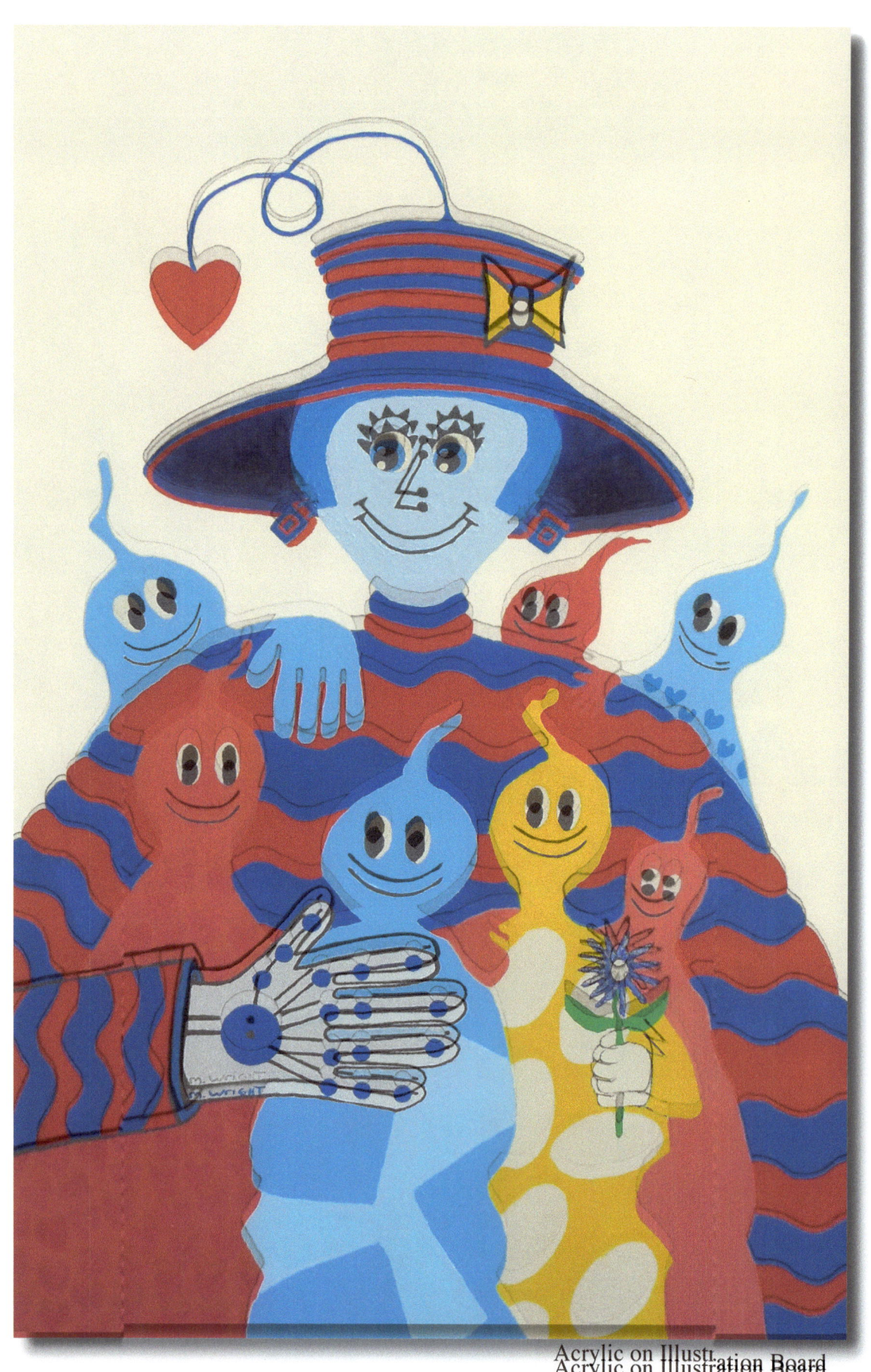

Acrylic on Illustration Board
20" X 30" - 1994

Gertrude Ghostbuster and Her Collection of Friendly Spirits

Gertrude Ghostbuster is a ghost-collecting robot. If your house is haunted, she will go through it collecting the ghosts, and when she leaves she will take all of them with her. After Gertrude Ghostbuster leaves each assignment, she takes the ghosts to places where they belong so they never need to haunt again. Ghosts cannot resist her loving nature, and they will follow her wherever she goes. She is shown here with her most recent followers who were all found in the same house. They were mischievous and kept the mortals up all night by giggling, moving the furniture, and banging on the piano. The mortals were extremely happy to see them leave and the ghosts knew they were going to a place where they were welcome, so everyone was happy.

The Great American Airhen

The Great American Airhen is large but it is very easy to operate. The operator pedals the big wheel to flap the wings, and pulls or lets out the cable attached to the beak. If the beak is high, the Airhen will gain altitude, so it needs a stable hand for consistent flight. When it is banking to come in for a landing, the operator pulls the beak down and instructs the passengers to move to the sides for stability. The Airhen needs a long runway, and wind speeds should be at least twenty miles per hour for it to operate efficiently. It uses no fuel, but it does require constant pedaling to stay in the air.

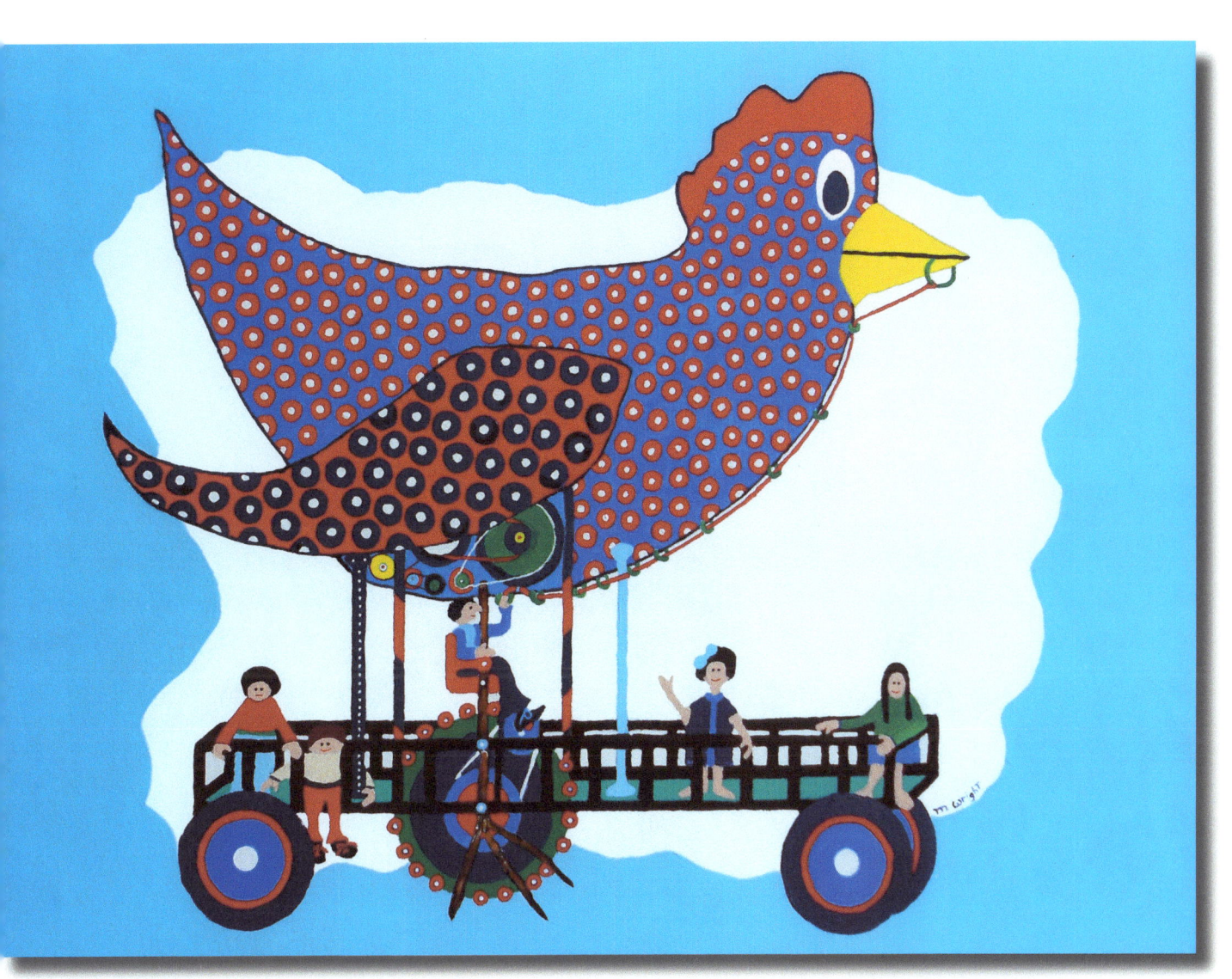

Acrylic on Canvas
28" X 38" - 1991

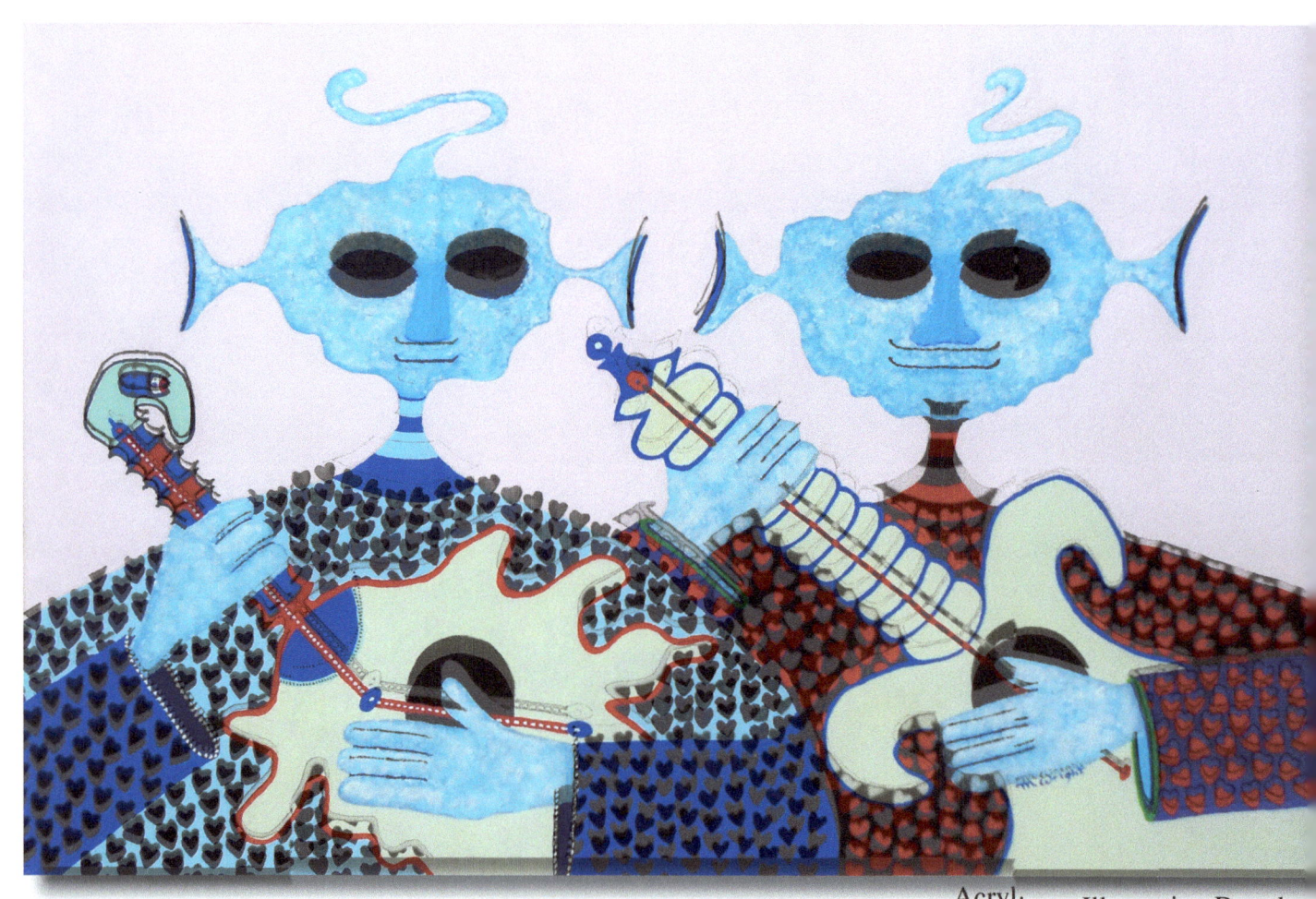

Acrylic on Illustration Board
20" X 30" - 1994

Jupiterian Musicians

I made this painting right after the comet hit Jupiter. At that time the people of Wyoming put an article in the *Rocky Mountain News*, inviting all Jupiterians made homeless by the comet to come to Wyoming. They stated that there is plenty of room in their state for newcomers and that the people of Wyoming are very hospitable and would welcome them eagerly.

This is a portrait of two of their musicians. Jupiterians are telepathic, communicating their thoughts through their antenna, but they can also hear. Earthlings would be able to hear their guitar-like instruments but would not be able to hear them chanting.

Jupiter is very far away and it is not known if the invitation from Wyoming has been received. In any case, it would take them a long time to make the journey to Earth, so we may not see them for many generations.

The Magical Mystical Mooch Machine

These pixies like to take small objects from your home when your back is turned. If you have ever left your glasses in the living room and returned later to find them gone, you might have been visited by these mischievous pixies. Their vehicle has been mooched too! The head came from a stick horse, the body was an old bolster from a couch, and the legs came from a stuffed animal. A discarded apron from an artist provides pockets where they put the purloined items.

The apron holds only a certain number of objects, so the pixies have to return them to make space for more. They have excellent memories and bring back what they have taken, but they seldom return the items to the place where they were picked up.

Eventually everyone is victimized by these pixies, so when this happens to you, just know that you are not alone. Eventually they will return the object they took, but rarely to the place where you left it.

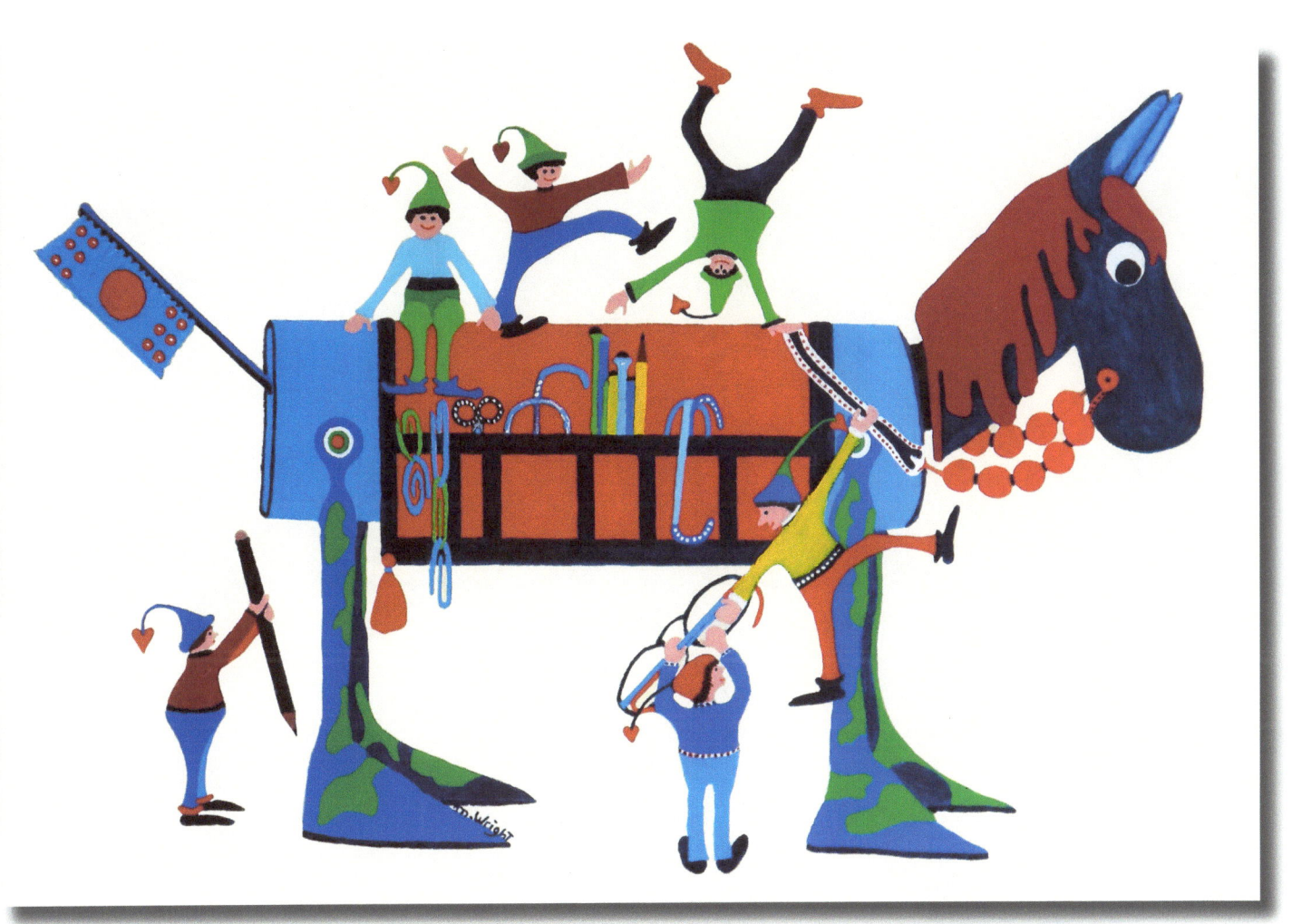

Acrylic on Canvas
24" X 36" - 1993

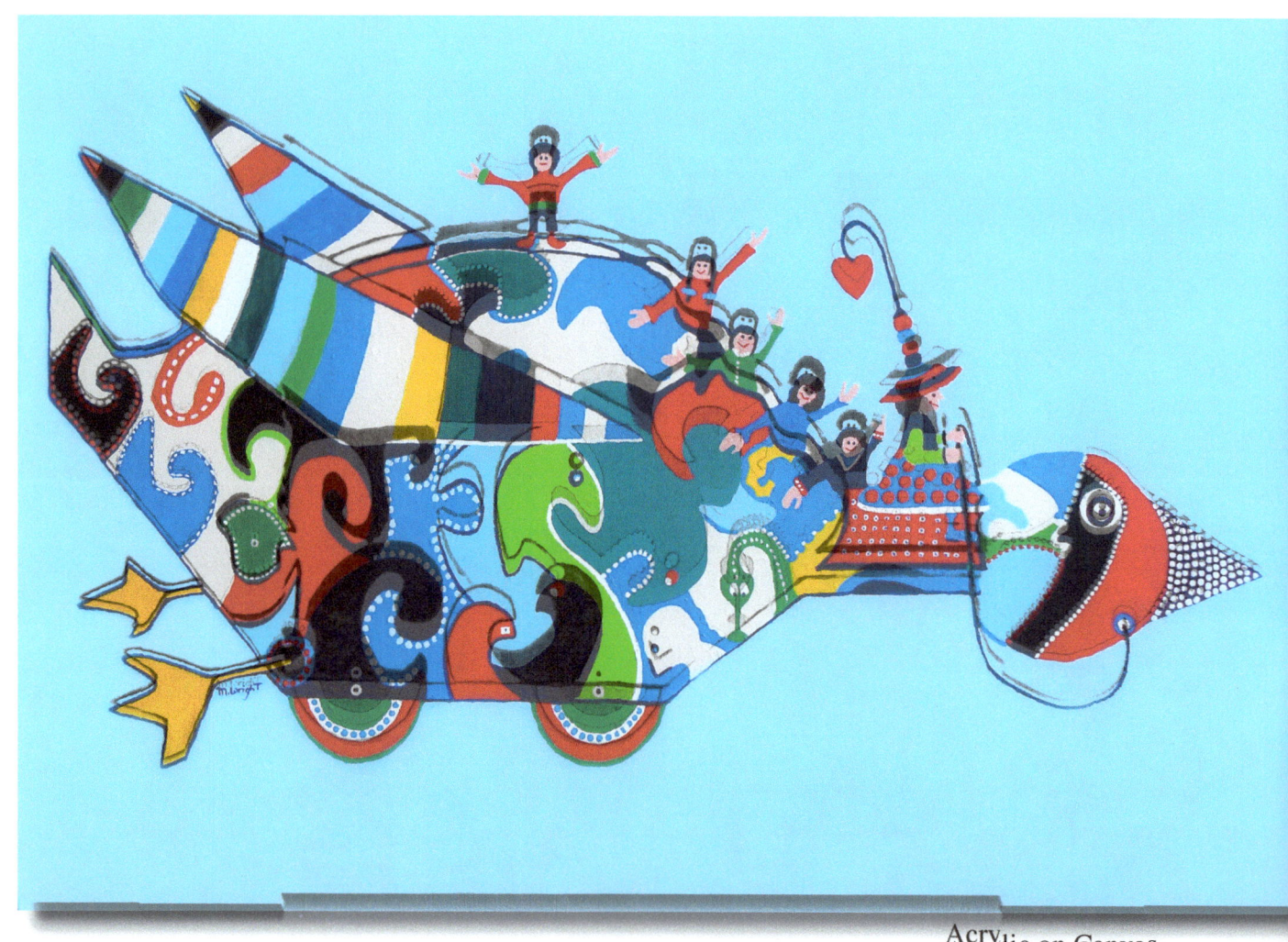

Acrylic on Canvas
24" x 36" - 2008

Mother Goose's Robot

I made this painting out of respect for Mother Goose and her demanding job. After all, taking small children for rides on the back of a goose has to be challenging! She doesn't take vacations, but her goose takes a leave of absence twice a year. Since geese are flocking birds they fly south together and take time off to raise their families, so Mother Goose is sometimes without transportation. She prefers to fly a live goose, but when one is not available she uses a robot.

Much Ado About Nothing

I named this painting "Much Ado About Nothing" because that is exactly what is happening! The figure on the lower left is pedaling his stationary car which turns the gears. Eventually all the gears will be spinning, but you will never see any results.

Sometimes life is like that! After you have put a lot of effort into a project, you find out that it was useless and that you had just been spinning your wheels.

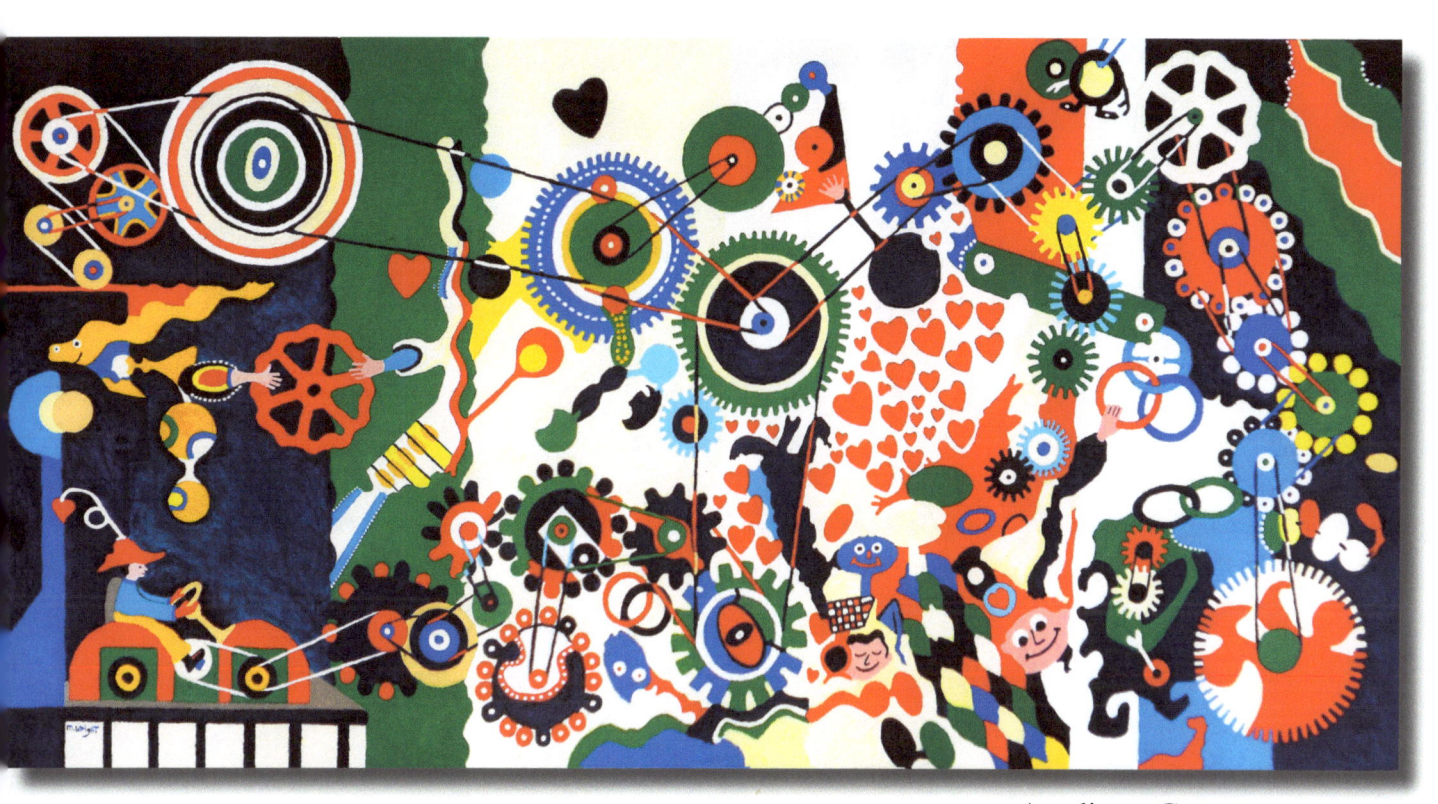

Acrylic on Canvas
24" X 48" - 2008

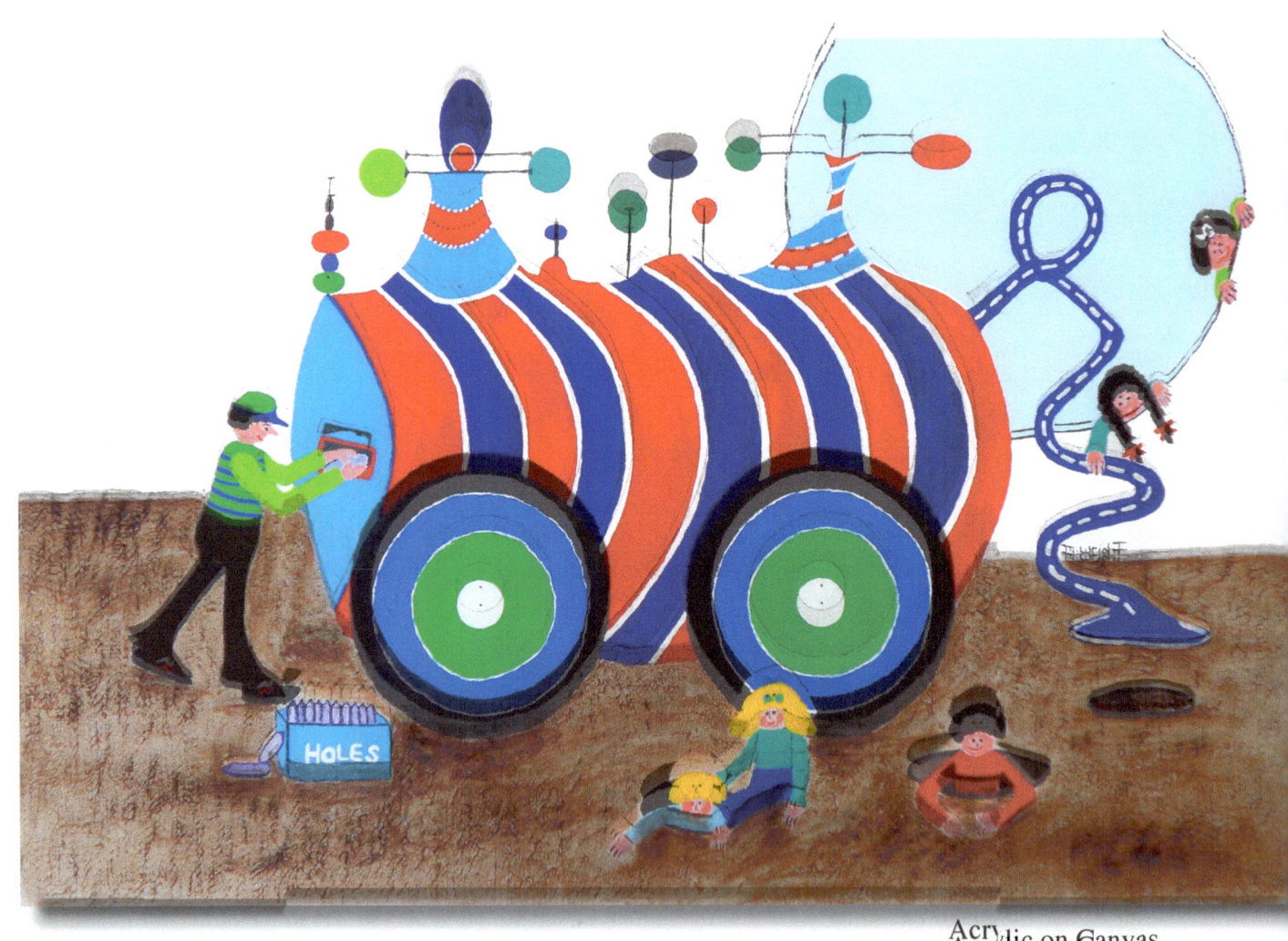

Acrylic on Canvas
24" x 36" - 1986

The Portable Hole Processor

This processor is designed to drop a hole wherever it is needed. Portable holes can be obtained in any size and are color coded to the dimensions of the hole they will make.

To use this machine, position it so the nozzle is over the area where you want your hole to be dropped. Place the unprocessed hole in the slot at the back, and be sure you are holding the nozzle with a firm grasp when the hole comes through. Holes exit the processor at high speed and are formed wherever they land, so be sure your feet are not under the nozzle.

Maintaining a hole processor is labor intensive, and improper handling of the chemicals inside could be injurious to your health. It is highly recommended that you rent a processor from your local holesale establishment.

Robot in Love with Vacuum Cleaner

This is a portrait of a housekeeping robot named Robettie Robott, who is programmed to clean your home until it is spotless. Her computerized brain enables her to make decisions about what to do and when to do it and she understands instructions well. Robettie Robott is a willing worker who never tires, but there is a problem. The programmer who designed and built her added a romantic side to her personality which has made problems for her and her humans. She has fallen in love with the vacuum cleaner, which she has named "Vic The Vac." He is only an upright plug-in, and the only way he can communicate with her is to put his cord around her shoulders, so the relationship is a little one sided. No one knows how long it will take Robettie Robott to realize that Vic The Vac is not the right mate for her, but right now she is so much in love that she is unable to work

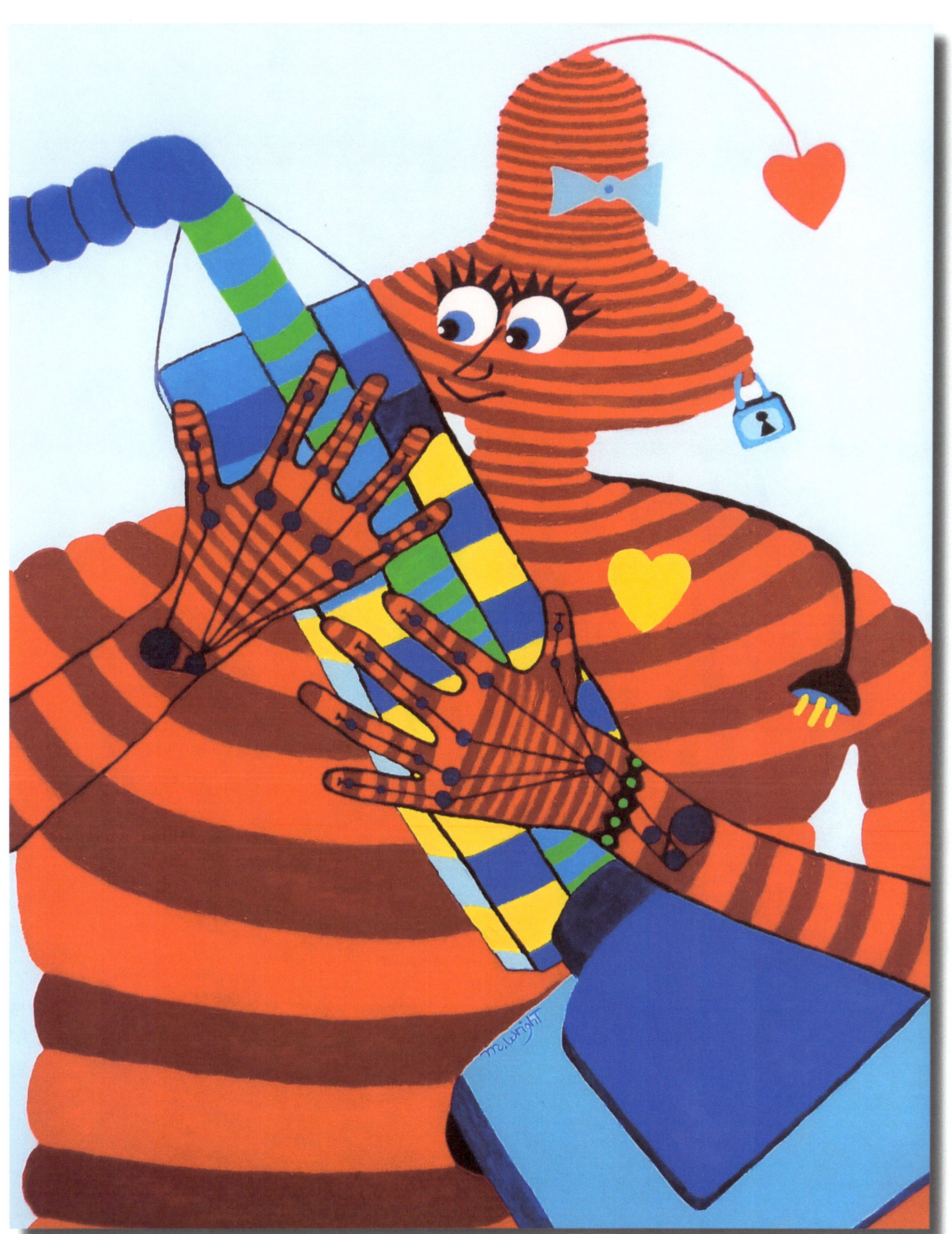

Acrylic on Illustration Board
22" X 30" - 1992

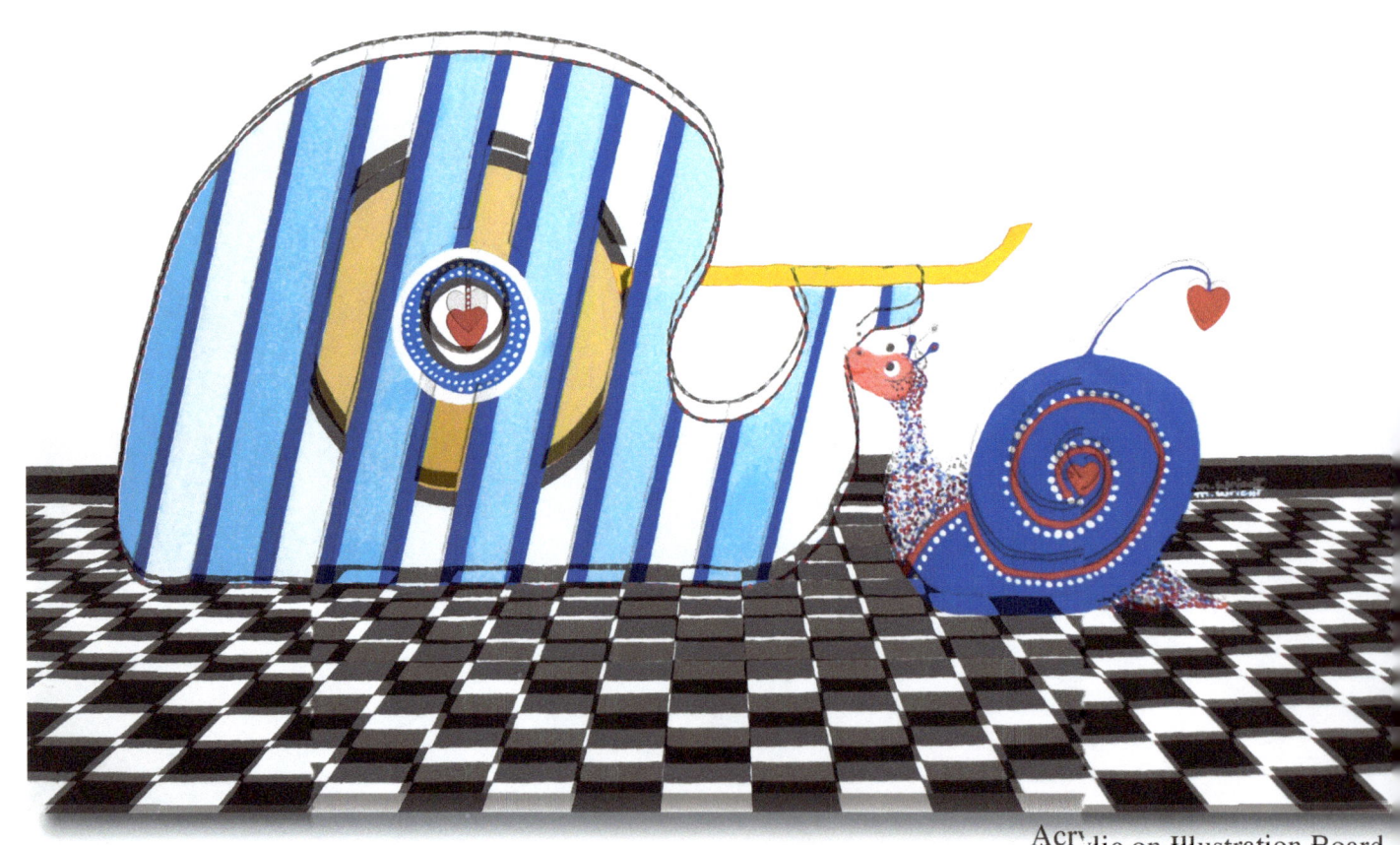

Acrylic on Illustration Board
20" x 30" - 2004

Snail in Love with Tape Dispenser

This romance began when a snail saw a tape dispenser on a table far above her head. Since the shape was similar to her own, she was sure it was another snail and wanted to get acquainted. The next morning she put on her best shell and began to crawl up the leg of the table. It took a long time for her to go up the leg, but when she arrived at the top she found that the object of her affection had not moved. At that moment she knew that he had waited for her, and instantly she fell in love with him and gave him a kiss on the neck. No one knows where this romance will go, but soon she will be more attached to him than she ever thought possible.

The Standing Assistance Machine for After a Nine Course Meal

This machine is known in medical circles as a "Postprandial Lifting Device." It is designed to help you to your feet if you have eaten too much and cannot stand alone.

After the meal the operator rolls the machine up behind the eater and places the hands under his arms so the fingers fit around his chest. There is a spring between the arms of the machine so the eater fits snugly in its grasp and cannot slip out and be injured. The operator then turns the crank at the back which operates the gears to raise the arms so the eater can be helped to his feet. The machine is designed with long arms so that when the eater stands, there is a space for the chair to be pushed back between him and the machine.

Standing assistance machines can be rented but they do not come with an operator. The renter is always responsible for hiring a designated non-eater, because if everybody eats a large meal, nobody stands.

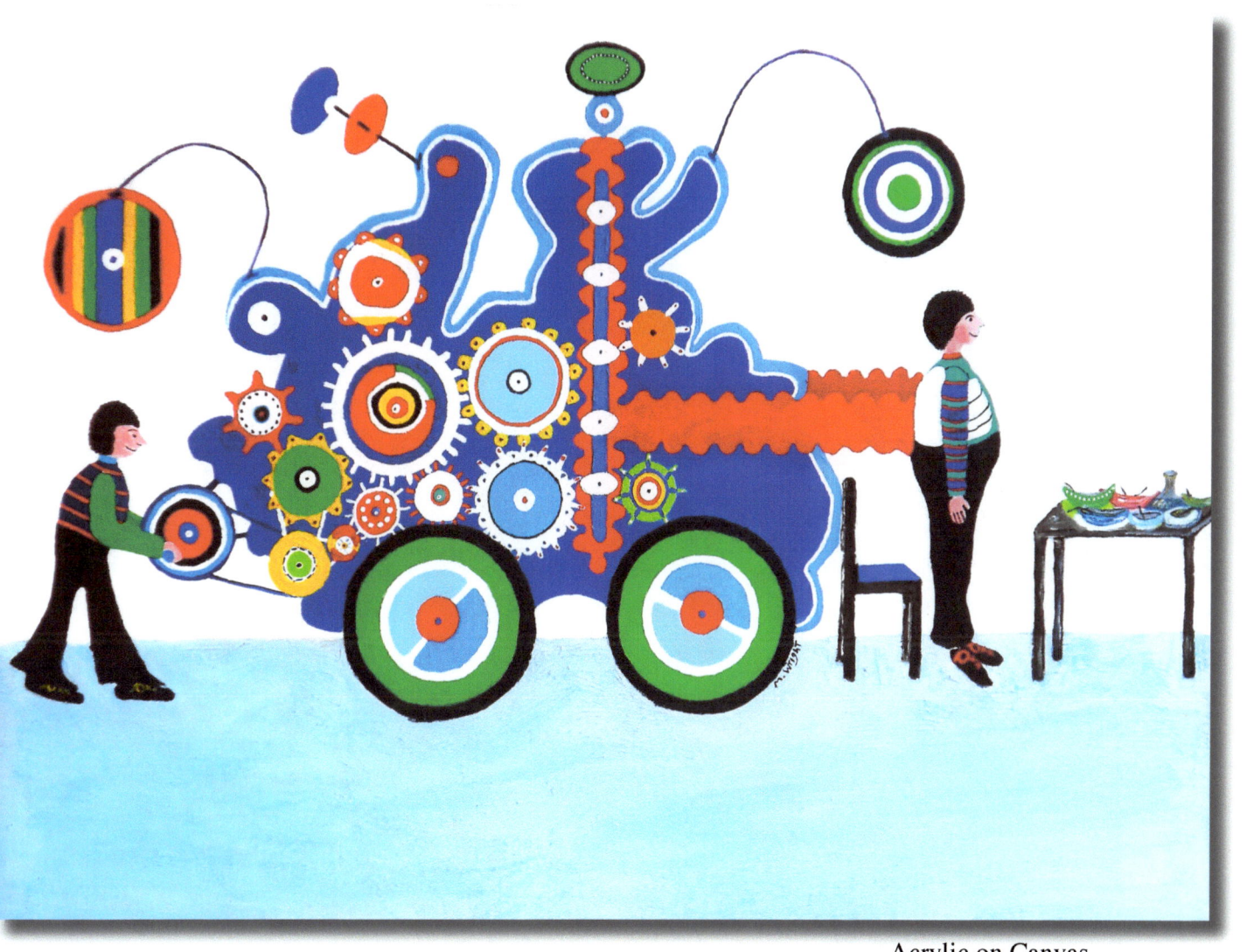

Acrylic on Canvas
26" X 36" - 1986

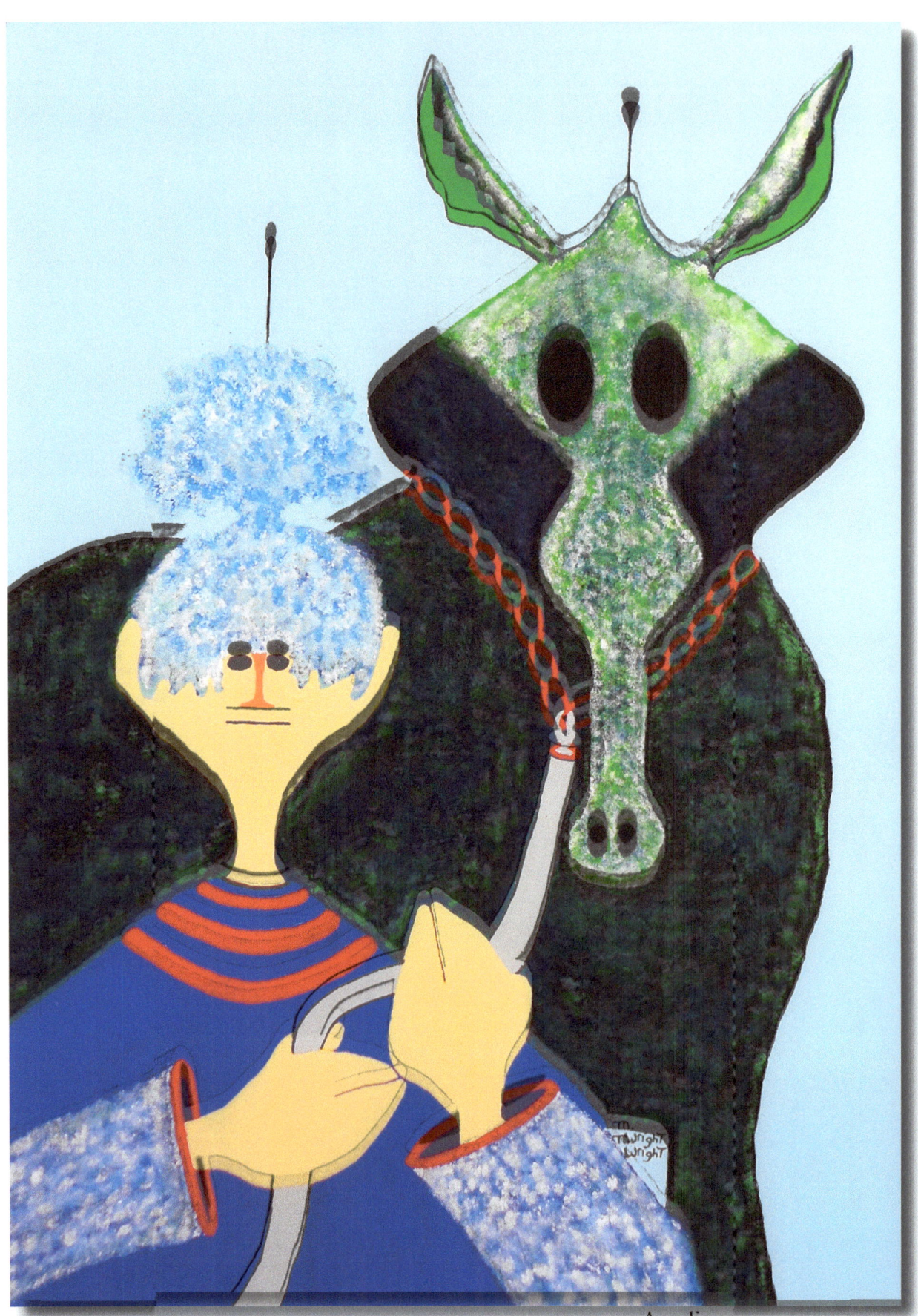

Acrylic on Canvas
25" X 32" - 1995

Teenager from Mercury with QPXMA

This is a portrait of a fourteen-year-old Mercurese female with her Grand Champion Qpxma, an animal that is extremely rare and exists only on Mercury. The snout is delicate so the Qpxma cannot be bridled and is handled by a collar around the neck. Qpxmas are docile and easy to train, but they are for show only and never used for food or as a beast of burden.

NOTE: Qpxma is pronounced "Kew-PIX-ema."

The Tuck in Kiss Goodnight Machine

This machine is for anyone who has not been tucked in and kissed goodnight recently. It fits over any bed from cot to king size, and is easy to operate.

When you are ready to sleep, get in bed and pull the machine toward yourself, being sure to lie down as it moves up the bed. When the machine is moving, the back wheels turn the gears which activate the arms to tuck the bedding in. On the front of the machine there is a wire face with a large fleshy mouth on the tip to kiss you good night, and at the same time a recorder in the back of the machine will play Brahms' Lullaby. Some people prefer to record the voice of a loved one telling them to sleep tight and not let the bugs bite.

Many who have used the Tuck-In Kiss Goodnight Machine say that it helped them sleep better, and that the next day they felt relaxed and ready to face the world.

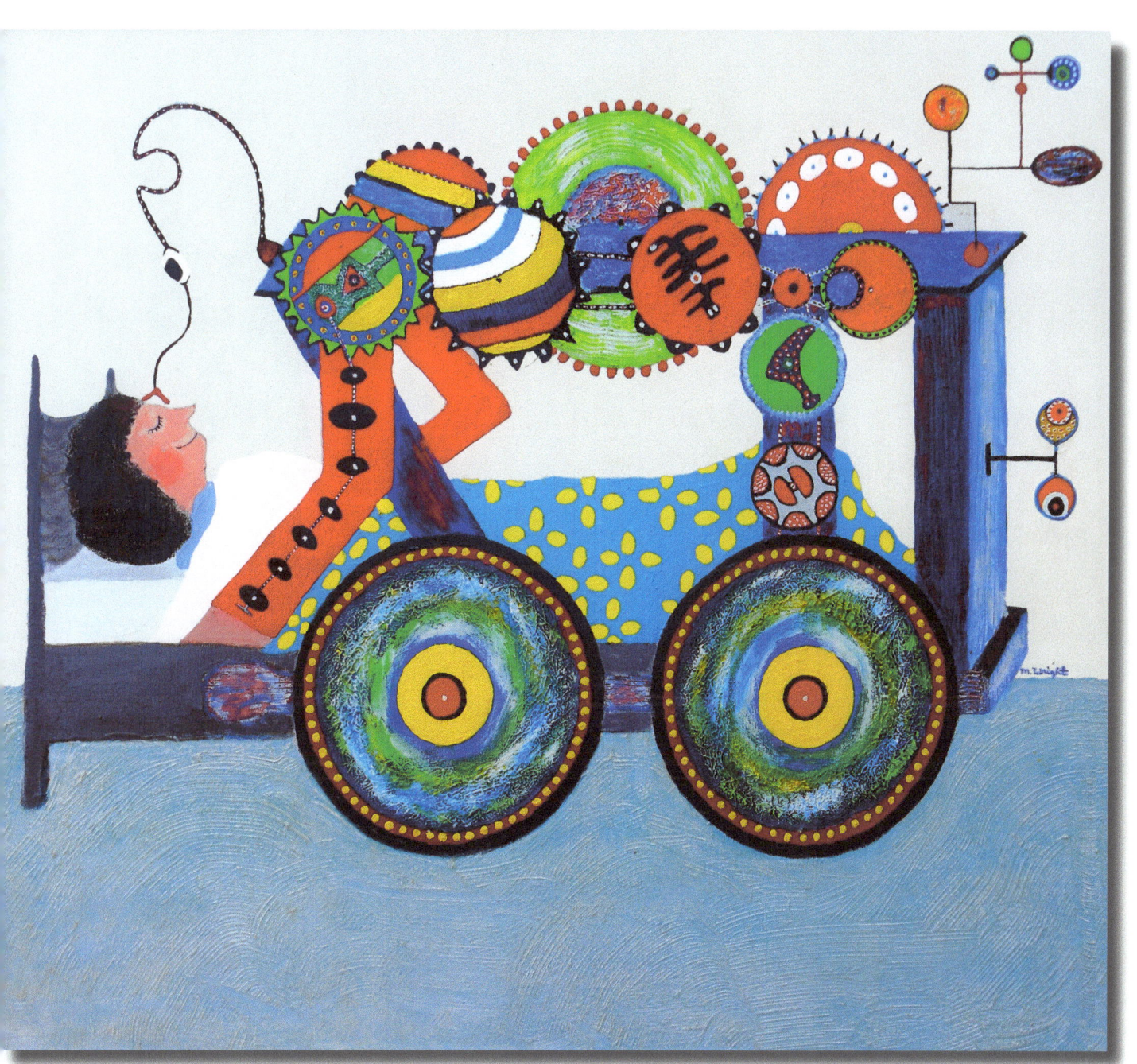

Acrylic on Canvas
30" X 34" - 1983

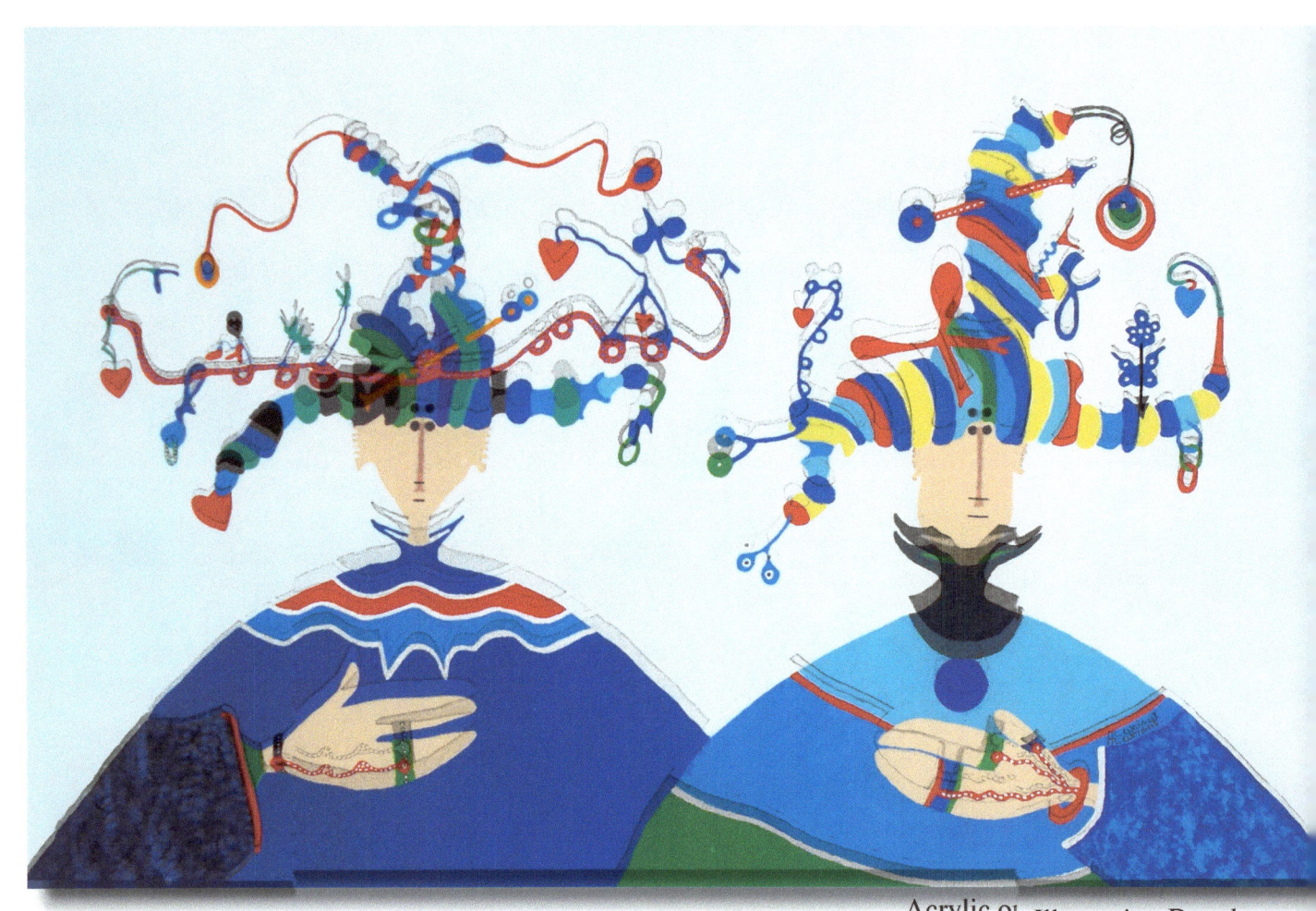

Acrylic on Illustration Board
20" X 30" - 1996

Two Women from Venus Wearing Elaborate Hats

Radiation on Venus is extremely high and as a result Venusians wear head coverings and long robes to protect their fragile bodies. Over time, exposure to the sun's rays has caused some genetic mutations so as a result they have elongated heads, long noses, and thin necks. Note also that they have only two fingers and a thumb on each hand.

Every year there is a contest to see who has the most elaborate hat, and this year these two women were the winner and runner up. On Venus it is the custom for them to have only one hand exposed. Venusian jewelry is worn on the hands and wrists and consists of a bracelet connected to one or two rings.

Woman Wearing Elegant Hat

This woman asked for her portrait to be painted wearing her newest, most elegant hat. She doesn't seem to mind that it is lob-sided, and it certainly will attract attention wherever she goes. One might also wonder where she would wear this hat, but that is her problem! She is happy with it and so is the milliner who made it because it was very expensive, and that is all that matters.

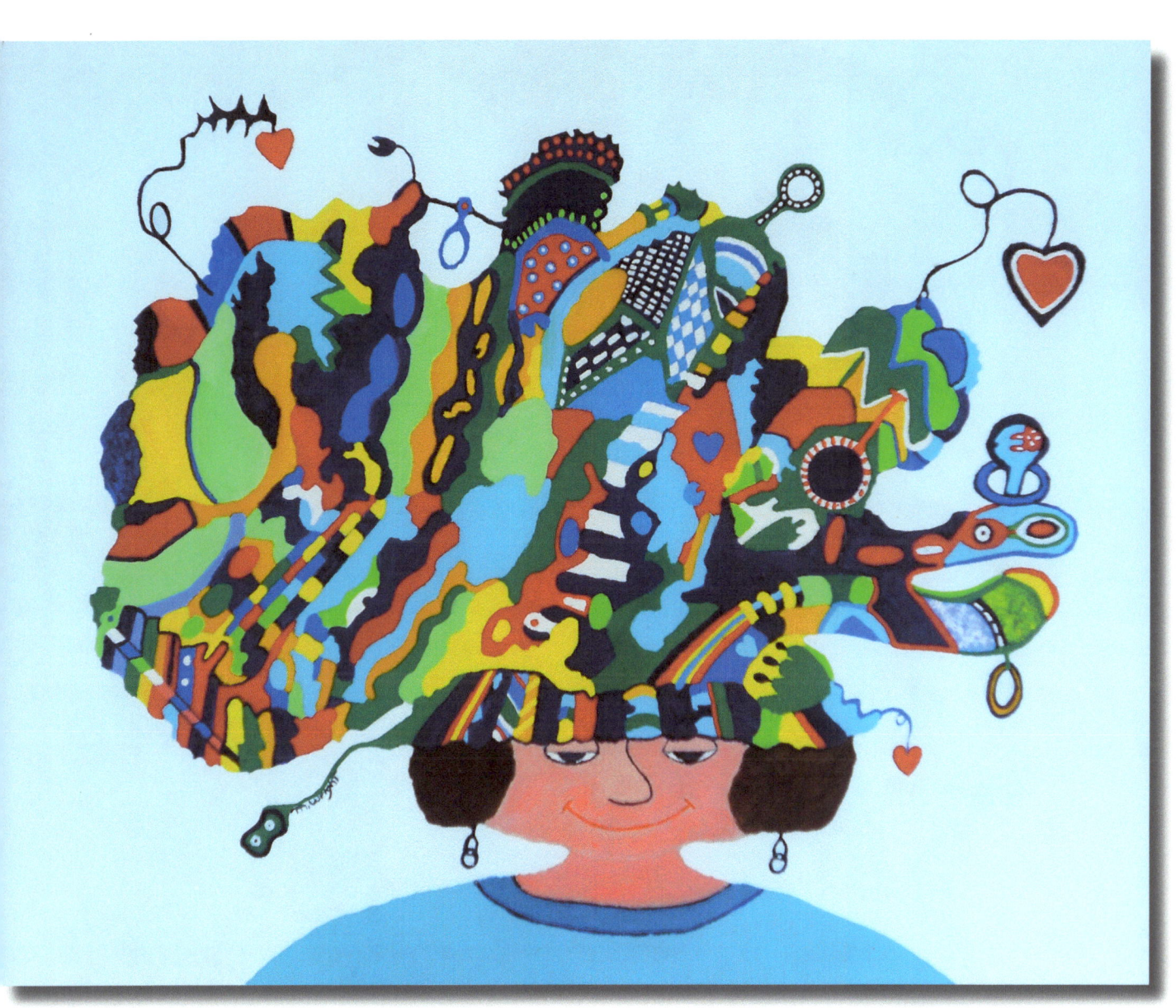

Acrylic on Canvas
24" X 36" - 2008

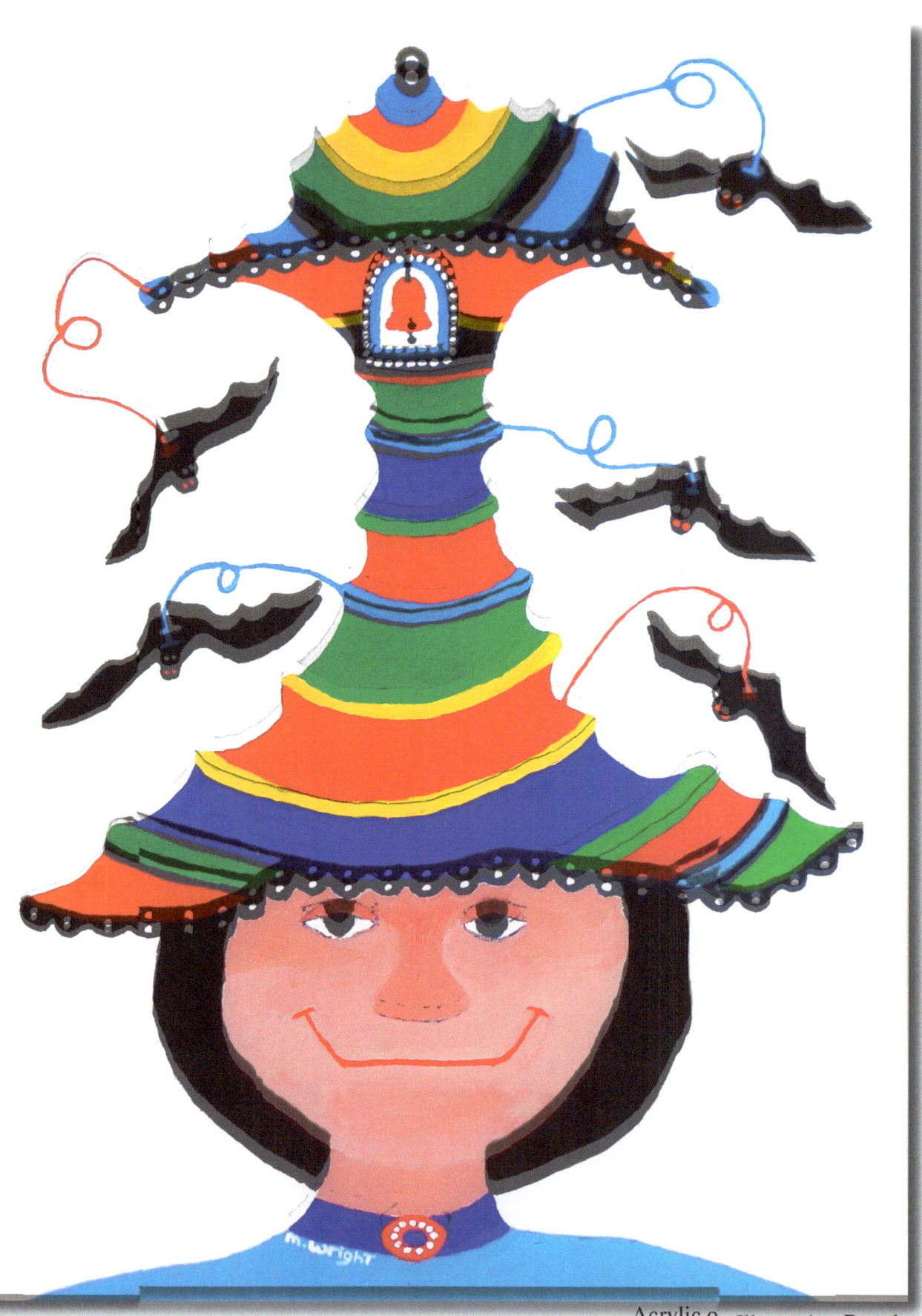

Acrylic on Illustration Board
20" X 15" - 2005

Woman with Bats in Belfry

This painting came from the expression my mother used to describe someone who was, as she put it, "a little funny in the head." I have always thought the expression "bats in the belfry" is descriptive, so I painted this woman with bats around her hat. Note that she also has a bell in her belfry. Apparently she likes the bats and they like her, but whatever is going on, the relationship has lasted a long time. No one really knows why unlikely attractions like these occur!

Woman with a Screw Loose

When I was a child I heard my father describe someone we knew as having a "screw loose." I thought that was a colorful description and wondered what a person with a loose screw might look like. This woman's helmet is covered with screws, but although the one on the top is coming unscrewed, the only loose one is on the right and about to fall out. Her friends, associates, and acquaintances will have plenty to talk about when she looses that screw!

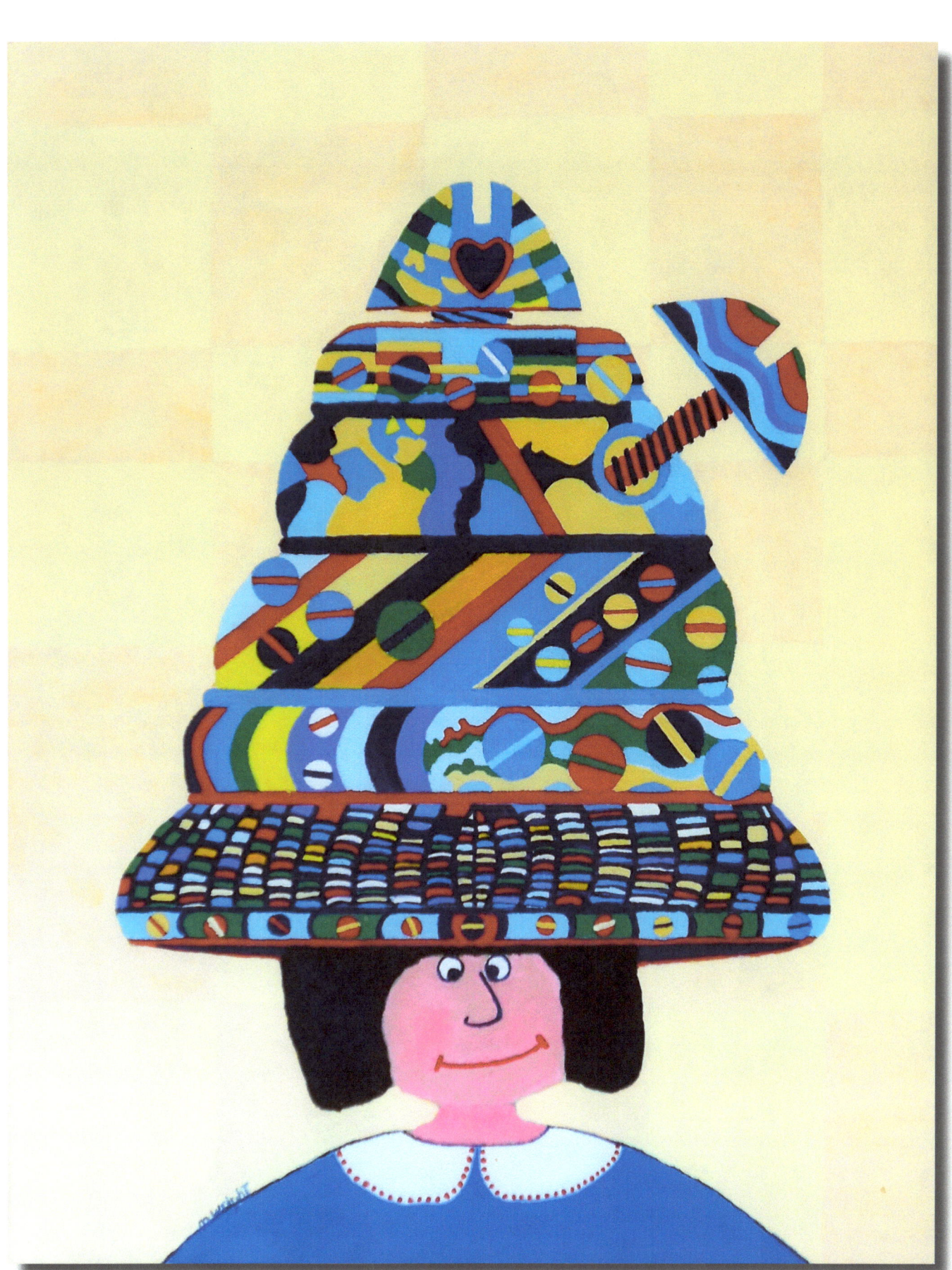

Acrylic on Canvas
22" X 30" - 2010

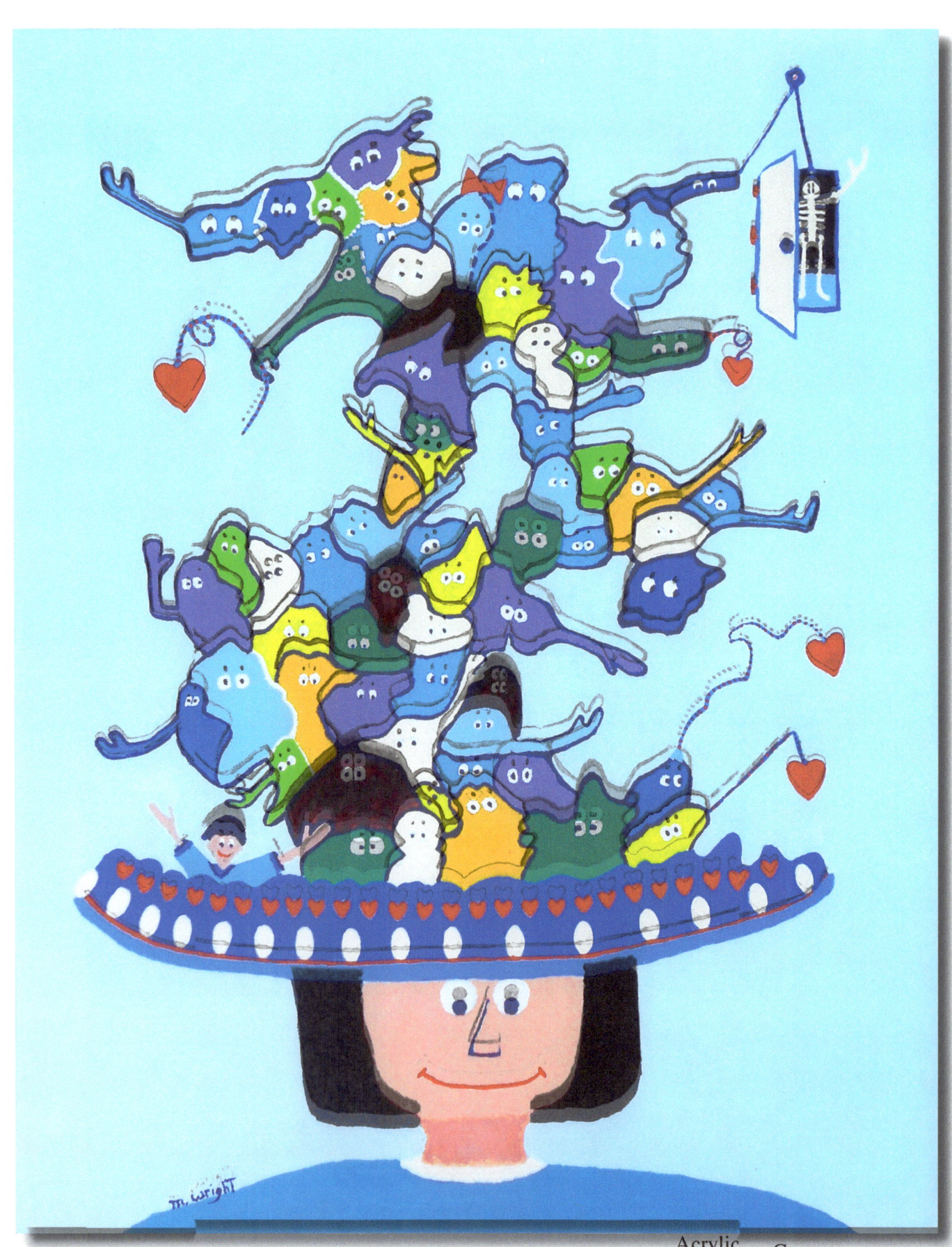

Acrylic on Canvas
22" X 28" - 2010

Woman with Skeleton in Closet

Just about everyone has at least one skeleton in their closet, and most people are reluctant to discuss it, but this woman does not mind exposing her skeleton and ghosts from the past for all to see. Please note that there is also a boy in her memories, but no one knows who he is or where he fits in. Just because someone reveals a skeleton in their closet and ghosts from the past doesn't mean they are willing to tell the world what it is all about.

Young Man with Hare on Chest

I made this painting for fun. No one knows why a hare would be on the chest of a four year old, but that is what came out of my paintbrush. Notice that the rabbit is quite dressed up, wearing an elaborate bow tie and dark pants and shoes, while the boy is in more casual attire.

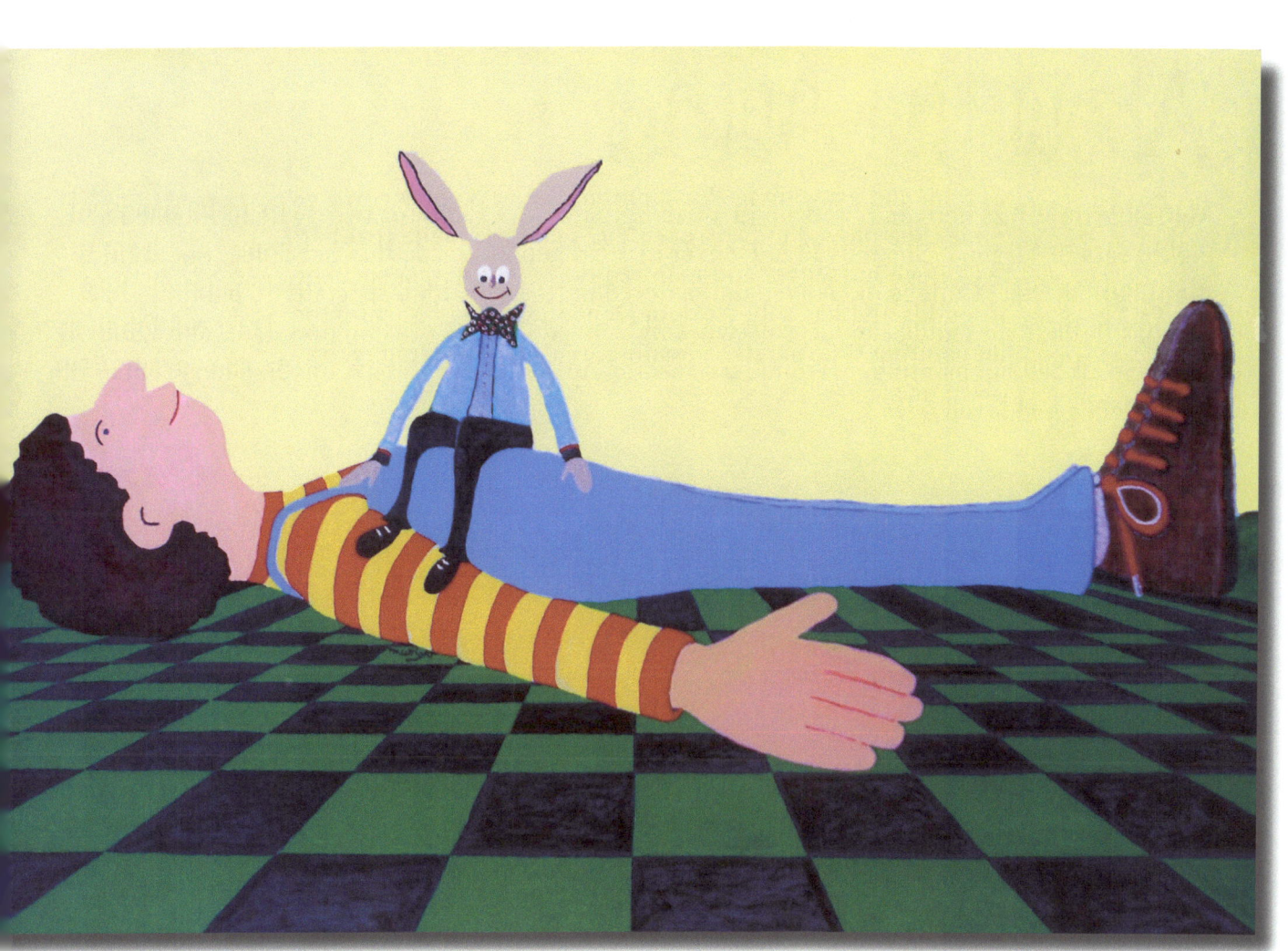

Acrylic on Illustration Board
20" X 30" - 2001

About the Author

Marion Wright was born and grew up in Washington, D.C. except for two years in England and eight years in Virginia. She moved to Denver in 1974 and has made that her home. She went to Metropolitan State College in Denver and majored in fine art with a specialty in painting. She belongs to three art guilds and has sold work in Denver, Omaha, Washington, D.C. and Edinburgh, Scotland. When not painting, Marion likes reading, music, photography, travel, and spending time with friends and loved ones.